B Foster.

EASTBOURNE

A Pictorial History

The bronze statue of Spencer Compton, 8th Duke of Devonshire, by Alfred Drury
(1856-1944) was erected on the Western Lawns in 1910, two years after the Duke's
death. The Duke was Mayor of Eastbourne in 1897-8, and the statue portrays him in the
robes of Chancellor of Cambridge University.

EASTBOURNE
A Pictorial History

D. Robert Elleray
Fellow of the Royal Society of Arts

Phillimore

First published in 1978

This edition published by
PHILLIMORE & CO. LTD.
Shopwyke Manor Barn, Chichester, West Sussex

1995

ISBN 0 85033 964 2

Printed and bound in Great Britain by
BIDDLES LTD.
Guildford, Surrey

For my daughter Lucy, with love

List of Illustrations

Frontispiece: Statue of the 8th Duke of Devonshire

Endpapers: Watering-places of England: Eastbourne, Sussex. *Illustrated London News,* 3 July 1852

Acknowledgements

I am indebted to the East Sussex County Library for permission to use material from the Local Collections at Eastbourne and Brighton Libraries. I am also grateful to the following for allowing me to copy photographs, drawings and other material: Eastbourne College, the *Eastbourne Herald*, Canon W.D. Giddey, John E. Goodwin, J. Leach, Father C. Spender, Stephen Tester, Mrs. M. Walkerley, Wright & Logan (Southsea) and Kenneth Young. I also thank the following for help, advice and comments received during my research: the Rev. D. Allen, M.A., Miss Elaine Baird, B.A., F.L.A., Mrs. Peggy Brown, C.R. Edgeley, the Eastbourne Natural History and Archaeology Society, J. Leach, Miss Sally Parsons, B.A., A.L.A. (Eastbourne Library), Leonard Stevens, the R.I.B.A. Library, Trinity House, the Transport and General Workers Union, and the Trustees of the Chatsworth Settlement.

The photographic work was carried out by Michael J. Coviello and John Tafft, and the MS prepared by Miss Esme Evans (Information Librarian, Worthing Library).

No watering place on the southern coast is fairer than Eastbourne; none is so elegant in the disposition of its attractions ... Eastbourne is indeed in all her attributes, a graceful dame, whose beauty is enhanced by every kind of becoming ornament.

The Daily Telegraph
14 December 1893

Introduction

The position of Eastbourne in the hierarchy of southern seaside resorts is presumed in the town's motto *Meliora Sequimur* adopted in 1858, and which seems to have become an incentive to achieve an ideal. During the next 30 years 'the best' was achieved, and in the 1880s the epithet 'Empress of Watering Places' had gained currency, while *Punch* found it appropriate to comment that the town was 'the Bourne to which all travellers return'. There is no doubt, however, of the seriousness of Eastbourne's claims to pre-eminence, or to question their basis in fact, and it seems fitting to preface any description of the town's development by some consideration of the principles and circumstances which caused Eastbourne to grow into the particular type of resort which it had become by the turn of the century.

From about 1775 until 1840, the area comprising the present town of Eastbourne saw a limited number of visitors seeking to enjoy the then quite novel custom of sea-bathing coupled with a period of residence on the coast, and in 1780 George III's children stayed for a time at the Round House. Because of these events there was a restricted development at Sea Houses, where a small fishing community had long been in existence, but no sudden growth followed, such as was the case at other suitable locations on the south coast, including Worthing and Brighton. The failure of Sea Houses to expand according to the familiar resort pattern of the period cannot be easily explained—and the reasons for it, as Dr. Peter Brandon remarks, 'remain speculative'.[1] Even so, there seems to be much in favour of ascribing the long periods of comparative inactivity, which extended well into the 19th century, to the particular nature of land ownership in the area. As a result, Eastbourne was never overwhelmed by unthinking development, but rather was in the enviable position of being able to choose the right moment to develop according to a considered plan. Writing at the beginning of the 20th century, George F. Chambers, in his delightfully discursive and informative *East Bourne Memories*,[2] hints at possible reasons underlying the town's delayed growth:

> The building all along the sea-front from the Grand Parade Westwards, which only began about 1860, or later, might have been started many years previously if the 1st Earl of Burlington had been favourable. I remember being shown once at *Compton Place* ... a complete and very comprehensive plan for a new town to be called 'Burlington', prepared in 1833 by a London architect of some repute, Decimus Burton. But Lord Burlington would have none of it: no bricks and mortar for him to disturb his privacy; so Burton went to Hastings and exploited the new town of 'St.-Leonards-on-Sea'.

From these considerations it seems that circumstances not only protected Eastbourne from unplanned, haphazard growth (as at Worthing), but also caused it to miss the urban Regency-style layout which came about at St Leonards, Hove, Kemp Town and elsewhere. Fortunately for Eastbourne, its final form was to embodied in an alternative which was an intelligent blend of both the 'rejected' forms—a well-mannered type of garden city fully exploiting the marine setting and the natural advantages of a varied and attractive landscape.

In 1935 the late Christopher Hussey[3] perceptively analysed the causes of Eastbourne's unique quality as a resort:

Academically considered, Eastbourne is a product of aristocracy: the outstanding example of a seaside resort developed consistently from the beginning 'according to plan'. Consequently its dominating impression on the ordinary visitor today (1935) is a friendly, spacious dignity. Historically it comes between the urban classic ideal realised in part at Brighton and St Leonards, and the modern conception of a garden city. As it grew, its character has been very much modified. There is evidence, in the original portions, of the influence of Decimus Burton at St Leonards [who later] turned from the idea of terraced streets to an orderly arrangement of detached houses in a well wooded layout, a policy soon adopted in Eastbourne. The key factor in this instance has been the ownership of the whole area by one, or rather two enlightened families. The Davies Gilbert Estate at the east end of the town shows no less foresight than the Cavendish Estate that comprises most of modern Eastbourne. To put one's finger on the precise point in space and time, the crucial decision that determined the character of Eastbourne, it may be suggested that the new town was conceived by a gentleman for gentlemen at a period when most development was being conducted by speculators for their own pockets.

The assertion of such enlightened policies, let alone their achievement, Hussey concludes, amounted to an idealism and balanced sense of values, rare, even unknown, in the mid-19th century. The implications of these unique beginnings have predictably influenced Eastbourne ever since and, together with the element of sustained and generous patronage by the Dukes of Devonshire, has meant that the town has had the resources to maintain a high standard of amenity—the benefits accruing from this ensuring the momentum of the resort's progress and prosperity. In practical terms these special circumstances enabled the town to avoid in large measure economic dependence on ordinary visitors, and one finds little evidence of the tendency to cater for the short-term holiday-maker, or 'tripper', to the detriment of the special quality of the resort's character. First-class entertainment has been consistently provided— a high standard set, and adhered to, leaving those with other tastes to go elsewhere if they so wished. As Harold Clunn,[4] writing in the period shortly after the First World War, nicely puts it: '[the town] ... Whilst extending a cordial welcome to the bona fide visitor and holiday-maker ... has never regarded the day tripper or the excursionist in any too kindly a light'—going on to note that: 'In days gone by the town used to petition the Railway Company not to issue any cheap day return tickets, calculated to attract any considerable crowd of excursionists to Eastbourne[!]'. This rather narrow idealism, if it ever existed to any large extent, has now been abandoned and any kind of discrimination become a thing of the past; yet the related ideal, that of maintaining the town as a well-planned and distinguished place both to visit and reside in, still, happily, persists to some degree. In this respect it is interesting to read in the *East Sussex County Structure Plan*[5] of 1975 that Eastbourne has '... a distinctive townscape, which is worthy of conservation, not so much because of the number of buildings listed as being of architectural or historic value, but rather because of the well-mannered, and spacious character'. Today Eastbourne, in company with many other towns, is experiencing the conflicts and pressures of change, growth and consequent development, inevitably putting at risk many of the attractive features of the town. Yet the major part of the Victorian resort, conceived with such idealism more than a century ago, survives, and in many ways has proved remarkably resilient in spite of the devastation of war and the insidious threat of mindless development. Put quite simply, Eastbourne has retained her *style*—and although inevitably subject to change, shows no sign of losing it: the 'spacious dignity' remains.

A Sketch of Eastbourne's Development Since 1780

In the middle of the 18th century the area now covered by the modern town of Eastbourne comprised four small and separate communities: the parent village of 'Bourne'[6] with its ancient parish church, subsequently referred to as the 'Old Town'; Southbourne, a single street extending south-eastwards some distance from Bourne towards the sea, centred on what is now South Street, while on the coast itself, near the present Splash Point, was the small fishing hamlet known since the 14th century as Sea Houses, and now surviving as Sea House in Marine Parade. Some distance to the west, on the slopes of Beachy Head, was the fourth settlement, the isolated hamlet of Meads. In the 1760s, when the attractions of the English coastline were being increasingly recognised and the benefit of sea-bathing as prescribed by Dr. Russell of Brighton was causing growing numbers of fashionable people to discover the seaside, it was at Sea Houses that the first visitors were received. Here accommodation was provided in the modest group of fishermen's houses, and it was these small buildings which became the embryo seaside resort of Eastbourne. The presence of visitors, however, soon caused improvements to be made in the area, and in Richard Gough's edition of Camden's *Britannia*[7] it is noted that 'Eastbourne, on the edge of Pevensey level, from a small dirty town, is much improved since it became a bathing place'. The somewhat scattered nature of Eastbourne at this period also draws comment, for in the *Guide to All the Watering and Sea-bathing Places* ...[8] there is reference to this characteristic: '... as the town [village] is at some distance from the shore, what are termed the sea-houses are chiefly frequented by company', adding that 'among the amusements of East Bourne may be reckoned the Circulating Library which was established here in 1795, and where there are also billiard rooms ...'. It appears that small covered baths were also available at Sea Houses, but it seems evident, in spite of Parry's remarks[9] that 'Eastbourne is a place of resort which we feel strongly inclined to recommend ... a genteel, yet small watering-place ...', the amenities then available must have left much to be desired—the library, baths and lodgings at the coast, the theatre some distance away in Southbourne, and the church and the *Lamb* assembly rooms even further removed in the village! Visitors to Sea Houses, however, do not seem to have been greatly deterred, and the growing popularity of the place is apparent from a report in the *Globe* in 1809: 'This little bathing place is thronged with families of the first distinction, not a house or even lodging can be obtained on any terms. The theatre is well attended ... the ball at the *Lamb Inn* on Monday boasted an overflow of fashionable company'.[10] Prominent among the buildings at Sea Houses was the 'Round House', said to be the surviving lower part of a mill, and converted into a marine residence some years before. It was to this building that George III's children came in the summer of 1780, with the consequent notoriety and increase in fashionable popularity which such visitations brought to several of the developing south coast resorts during the period. Of this important event George F. Chambers remarks that the visit '... may be said to mark the starting of the town as a bathing and pleasure centre ...'.[11] But possibly for the reasons already referred to, there was no rapid increase in the size of Sea Houses, and some sixty years or more were to pass before the four scattered areas were amalgamated into the resort of Eastbourne.

An important element in the background to Eastbourne's history during the late 18th century and the opening years of the 19th century were the wars on the nearby Continent, and the very real threat of invasion by Napoleon's armies. These conflicts, although producing negative conditions nationally, had a positive aspect with regard to the English resorts and spas, causing people who would have normally gone abroad to find their amusements and relaxation to stay and explore their own country during the war years. As a result of the Napoleonic threat, and especially following the renewal of hostilities in 1803, Eastbourne found itself within the area designated by the Government for the erection of a line of manned coastal defences—the series of famous Martello Towers, the most westerly but one of which was the Wish Tower. In addition, one of the two major forts (the other was at Dymchurch) in the system, the Redoubt, was erected a little east of Sea Houses. These forts, together with numerous camps, caused a significant influx of troops with their dependents into the area, which led to a period of local prosperity. Conversely, however, when the crisis ended in 1815, the subsequent demobilisation was followed by depression and unemployment.

The economic stagnation which followed the Napoleonic Wars persisted well into the 19th century, and perhaps a result of these conditions in Eastbourne was the persistence of the most simple form of local government—a Vestry Meeting—which consisted of representatives chosen by the local Justices. This basically rural system continued until the first moves to develop the town on modern lines began in around 1850, and in 1858 advantage was taken of the newly-passed Local Government Act to establish a Local Board, for which elections took place on 14 January 1859. George F. Chambers[12] writes of the first Board that it was 'fairly representative of all classes (including) ... the Vicar, 2 Magistrates, 1 Barrister, 3 Doctors, 1 Builder, 1 Butcher, 1 Watchmaker, 1 Upholsterer, 3 Brewers, 1 Innkeeper, 1 Miller, 6 Farmers, and 2 private residents, one of whom was a gentleman and the other who was not'. An immediate need of the new Board was for an Official Seal, and this was prepared by the Sussex antiquarian M.A. Lower. The resulting design combined elements from the coats of arms of the three main families connected with the town's history—a shield, antlers and a rose—representing Badlesmere (baronial holders of the lordship of Eastbourne c.1300), Cavendish and Gilbert in that order. To this Lower added a seahorse, symbolising the town's marine situation, and supplied the motto *Meliora Sequimur*, which he chose as 'appropriate to the public spirit of the townsmen ... and calculated to advance the interests of your deservedly popular watering-place'. It is recorded that Mr. Lower received a gratuity of three guineas for his trouble!

The year 1858 saw another event of the greatest importance in Eastbourne's history— the succession of William, 2nd Earl of Burlington, then resident at Compton Place, to the Dukedom of Devonshire, thus becoming the 7th Duke. At this time the area of the 'town', some 6,000 acres (11,356 in 1990), was divided between the Cavendishes and the Gilberts, the first centred on Compton Place, the second in the Old Town area, this large tract of private land creating an effective block to rapid change. It was the decision of these two governing families to begin an orderly development of their Eastbourne estates during the years 1850-1860 that radically changed the prevailing status quo in the town. Some growth had, however, begun to occur before 1858; in 1837, the need for additional church accommodation nearer Sea Houses and Southbourne had been felt, resulting in the erection of a Chapel of Ease (Trinity Chapel) on open land between the two communities. The chapel was soon enlarged and given parish status in 1847. Two years later a branch railway was opened to Eastbourne from Polegate, and a station established between the Old Town and Southbourne. The arrival of the railway was well timed to play a vital rôle in the development anticipated by the Earl of Burlington, and the station formed a nucleus of new growth, the first stage of which was the construction of Terminus Road linking the railhead with Sea Houses and bypassing the old indirect route via Southbourne (South Street). These new developments south-east of the Old Town led to a marked distinction between the coastal area and the old village—between the old and the new Eastbourne— leading progressively to a decline in the importance of the Old Town. This tendency was

1 William, 7th Duke of Devonshire (1808-1891) has been aptly described as chief benefactor and founder of modern Eastbourne. In 1858, as 2nd Earl of Burlington, he succeeded to the Dukedom and exercised a controlling and enlightened influence on the town's development.

emphasised in 1851 when the seat of local administration, the new Vestry Room, was erected near the station in Grove Road.

In retrospect the decade 1850-1860 may be seen as the period of transition from the old to the new, and it appears that the beginnings of development which occurred during these years were accompanied by some uncertainty. J.C. Wright[13] states that the foundation of the new Eastbourne began in the spring of 1851, naming Edward Maynard as the chief pioneer, together with James Peerless, Thomas Wilmot, and John Gosden, who built Cornfield Terrace. At the same time Maynard was building in Seaside Road, Terminus Road and the east side of Cornfield Road. These operations were encouraged by the Earl of Burlington who gave financial assistance in the shape of 75 per cent advances of capital sums required. The importance of the sea-front as a key section of the new resort was recognised by the Earl, and the surveyor and architect James Berry was specially appointed to survey and lay out the main portion of the Parade in 1847. This preliminary spate of building, however, turned out to be somewhat premature; houses went up, but in many cases tenants were not forthcoming and several developers found themselves in financial difficulties. As a result a number of sites and new properties reverted to the Duke, who, in turn failing to dispose of them, had recourse to selling by auction, this being done at the *Ship Hotel*, Brighton in August 1859.

Following this early setback, however, the development of modern Eastbourne made rapid strides; the next decade witnessing a near doubling of the population from 5,795 (1861) to 10,302 (1871) and, as already indicated, the expansion went forward as a well-planned campaign, the basic requirements such as adequate drainage, roads and water supply being provided at the outset.

By 1881, when the major phase of the town's growth was at its height and the population had again doubled, *The Times* accurately commented: 'To effect all this, two things chiefly have been demanded—namely, public spirit and capital. This spirit has been evinced and the capital expended by the Duke of Devonshire, who owns a large part of

Eastbourne, and who has expended about £300,000 on drainage, roadworking, forming the parade, and in generally improving the town—all of which improvements he has freely dedicated to the public service'. During the period many of the characteristic buildings and institutions of Eastbourne had come into existence. The number of churches had steadily increased: Christ Church, Seaside in 1859, and the distinctive church of St Saviour in 1867, with its tall stone spire becoming a noble landmark in the town. A decade later, in 1883, one of the most spectacular Victorian churches in Sussex, All Souls', Susans Road, was erected, financed by Lady Veronica Long Wellesley on land presented by the Duke of Devonshire. Even more note-worthy than the church building in the town, however, was the extraordinary number of schools which established themselves in the area, the most notable of these being Eastbourne College, founded in 1867. Another important foundation in the town at this time was that of All Saints' Convalescent Home, which, with its exceptionally fine and little-known chapel, forms one of the most interesting groups of Victorian architecture in the town. The last quarter of the 19th century saw the development of the Upperton area with the erection of the Gilbert Estate, including St Anne's church, set in the elegant Upperton Gardens, and the Princess Alice Memorial Hospital (1883), in Carew Road. By this time Meads, once enthusiastically described as the 'Belgravia of Eastbourne', was also being incorporated into the town, and its elevated situation soon made it a most attractive residential area and an ideal location for convalescence and education.

By the 1870s the possibility of the Incorporation of the town was being widely discussed and, when in 1883 the population topped 22,000, the Local Board successfully applied for a Charter. George F. Chambers[14] summarises the local feeling concerning Incorporation as follows: '[It] was really the outcome of the steady growth of public opinion that the town ought to go ahead, and that a new Governing Body of go-ahead men was needed. The 'do-nothings' viewed the scheme of a Charter with great disfavour, but they were powerless to stem the flowing tide'. The election of the first Council took place on 1 November 1883; George A. Wallis, the Duke of Devonshire's agent and last Chairman of the Local Board, became the town's first Mayor. Following some acrimonious differences of opinion over the choice of a site, a Town Hall was erected and opened in Grove Road in 1886. By the time of Incorporation the town was already providing an excellent range and variety of resort amenities. A pier designed by Eugenius Birch had been completed in 1872, followed by the Saffrons Cricket and Football Ground in 1886, but Eastbourne's greatest attraction

2 George Frederick Chambers, barrister, local historian and amateur astronomer, played an important part in the town's affairs during the Victorian period. He was elected to the first Town Council in 1883, and later wrote *East Bourne Memories* and several other books, including a standard guide to the district which remained in print for several years.

was Devonshire Park which opened in 1874. Laid out on land given by the Duke, it provided a Winter Garden besides including many sports facilities—roller-skating, croquet and especially tennis courts. In 1884 Devonshire Park Theatre was added, which has remained one of the town's main attractions ever since. Seaside and Seaside Road became a centre for popular entertainment—the Theatre Royal and Opera House (Hippodrome) opened in 1883, followed later by four cinemas, Mansell's (Tivoli), Central, Eastern and Elysium, all now closed but with façades still surviving in 1994. But it was the importance given to music which was to prove the most remarkable element in Eastbourne's entertainment, beginning with the Duke of Devonshire's Orchestra founded in 1874, and later the promotion of an annual Music Festival which drew many famous performers and conductors to the town. An important result of the high standard of municipal entertainment, added to the climatic and scenic advantages and the excellent hotels, was the seasonal influx of distinguished visitors. Compton Place on a number of occasions provided accommodation for royalty, and in addition many notable writers, musicians, scientists and politicians found enjoyment and relaxation in common with those who came to partake of the traditional benefits of the town as a fashionable health resort.

In 1900, with the population approaching 43,000, the rate of the town's growth was beginning to level off, and in 1906 the first and unsuccessful application was made by the town for County Borough status. In 1911, however, a second application was made and succeeded, the new boundaries including part of Willingdon. In 1900 the purchase of Hampden Park by the Borough was completed, and the following years saw the erection of the Technical Institute (1904), the laying-out of the Redoubt gardens, the purchase of Gildredge Park, and the gift of Motcombe Gardens to the town by the 8th Duke of Devonshire.

During the First World War a reasonable measure of prosperity was enjoyed by the town, stemming mainly from numerous visitors and a considerable influx of war convalescents and service personnel. These were concentrated in the large Summersdown Camp near the Golf Links; in addition, a Cavalry Command Depot was set up in Victoria Drive and an aerodrome established near St Anthony's Hill. Between Polegate and Lower Willingdon an airship station was constructed which maintained anti-submarine patrols over the adjacent areas of the Channel.

The period between the wars was not marked by any great expansion, a circumstance reflected in the level of population which remained around 57,000 over the period 1920-1939. This state of affairs was somewhat different from other resorts, notably Worthing, where because speculative housing development was unimpeded the same years witnessed a near doubling of population. However, some housing estates were being built, beginning with Seaside and the Old Town in 1919, and later at Hampden Park. The problems of town planning and conservation were beginning to be recognised, for in 1931 the *Eastbourne and District Regional Planning Scheme* was published, while during the same period the important step of preserving the town's downland setting, including Beachy Head, was taken. In spite of these positive moves, one area of Eastbourne remained neglected: the Old Town. Here haphazard demolitions in connection with attempts to widen the High Street led to the loss of several historic buildings, and the changes which began at this time have unfortunately persisted and, following the demolition of the Star Brewery in 1973, the decision to erect a supermarket on the site continued the 'damage' in this historic area. One old building to survive, at least in its external appearance, was the Manor House opposite the *Lamb Inn*, which in 1923 was turned into the Towner Art Gallery and has become one of the best art exhibition centres in Sussex. Developments connected with the resort during the inter-war years included the new concert pavilion on the pier (1924-5), the erection of the central bandstand, Grand Parade (1935), additional cinemas, the building of a large brick church, St Elizabeth's, in Victoria Drive, and the completion of the Roman Catholic Church of Our Lady of Ransom near the Town Hall. A new open space, Princes Park, was laid out at the eastern end of the town and provided a lake formed from the old Crumbles Road. Following the acquisition of the Redoubt by the Borough, a bandstand (later demolished) was established on the west side of the fort. At the other end of the town, the old chalk quarry at Holywell was transformed into a pleasant sunken garden with sheltered lawns and a tea pavilion. The importance of Devonshire Park was maintained and its major buildings were purchased by the town in the 1930s, this transaction once more indicating the Park's important rôle in the town's economy—a point emphasised earlier in 1912, when, during council discussions concerning proposed purchase, the Park was described as 'the sheet anchor of Eastbourne's prosperity'.

The Second World War and After

In 1939 Eastbourne was about to enter a period when its existence and prosperity were to be endangered by war. This had happened before in the years around 1805, but what remained a threat during the Napoleonic Wars turned into a grim reality in 1940-5, when the town suffered both social upheaval and extensive damage and casualties owing to enemy air attack. Some idea of the severity of these raids is evident from the fact that 200 people were killed, 1,289 injured and 1,475 buildings destroyed or badly damaged. The autumn of 1939 saw the town increasingly congested by evacuees, and for a time it seemed that some prosperity would result. These hopes proved short-lived, however, for in May 1940, when France capitulated and invasion was considered imminent, the town found itself very much in the front line. First the London school-children and visitors were re-evacuated, and then in September 1940 a general evacuation was ordered, many of the people going to reception areas in Gloucestershire. Eastbourne was left with a population of about 27,000, many of these being service personnel stationed in the area, such as the naval unit HMS *Marlborough*, which occupied Eastbourne College. After a lull in the air raids late in 1941, the period from May 1942 until mid-1943 saw the town subjected to frequent 'hit-and-run' attacks and later flying bombs, which devastated many areas and destroyed several notable buildings such as the Technical Institute and Library, the churches of St John's, Meads (rebuilt 1957), and St Anne's, Upperton Gardens.

By the end of the war conditions in the town were so bad that the task of reconstruction and rehabilitation was of major proportions, the pier alone costing some £80,000 to restore. The prime objective of repairing damaged housing and that destroyed was pursued as rapidly as the difficult post-war conditions allowed. Priority was also given to the re-opening of hotels and boarding houses, with the aim of effecting an early reinstatement of the town's resort trade. Generally these objectives were achieved but, as in many other parts of England, the experience of war caused a break with the past which could never quite be healed. The demand for housing led to new large-scale estate developments by the Local Authority in the Old Town, Hampden Park and, later, Langney areas. To these activities were added building programmes undertaken by the Chatsworth Estates Company, the combined effect of this expansion being a marked change in the appearance of Eastbourne outside the limits of the Victorian town. The time was becoming ripe for 'developers', and by the late 1950s their activities were beginning to produce changes not always in the best interests of the town's appearance.

Connected with the Borough's policy to stimulate and foster every aspect of the town's function as a leading resort was the attention given to the idea of making Eastbourne a 'conference centre'. To this end the ambitious plan for erecting the Congress Theatre as part of the Devonshire Park complex was brought to fruition in 1962-3, and the idea of creating a building with the dual purpose of conference hall/theatre and concert auditorium has continued and supplemented the best tradition of the Park in the sphere of entertainment.

The decade 1950-1960 saw an increase in Eastbourne's population of only some 2,000 people, but the next ten years witnessed a quite dramatic jump of nearly 11,000, a figure reminiscent of the town's golden age of growth in the latter part of the 19th century. The entirely new departure of introducing a trading estate for light industry also came about during this period, with the development at Brampton Road near Hampden Park railway station, where building began with the Armour Laboratory. The year 1971 was marked by the exceptionally high housing figures achieved by the town—371 new dwellings built, and 1,490 under construction—a total exceeded only by Croydon in the whole country. Steady growth has continued and by 1994 the population had reached 83,400. The environmental cost of this expansion has been considerable—the consolidation of the ribbon development along the A22 northwards, and the encroachment on the 'levels', a sensitive area vital to the survival of the town's natural setting. The massive developments in the Langney area with the Crumbles village and harbour has virtually destroyed the natural environment to the east of the town in a similar manner to the destruction of Blackrock at Brighton by the Marina.

In the Victorian areas of the resort, however, and especially on the sea-front, there seems to be every chance that the 'well-mannered and spacious character' referred to in the Structure Plans will survive despite the incursions of the high-rise South Cliff Tower (1966) and the T.G.W.U. Conference Centre (1975). Other unfortunate lapses have been the high-rise developments along the Upperton Road, Ripley Chase in the Goffs and the destruction of St Peter's church, Meads Road. More positively the economic and social benefits resulting from the well designed Arndale Centre (1981) have been considerable and further enhanced the already high reputation of Eastbourne as a resort of exceptional quality and resource.

D. ROBERT ELLERAY
1995

Notes

1. *The Sussex Landscape* (1974), p.255.
2. 1912, p.36.
3. *Country Life*, February 1935, p.135.
4. Clunn, H., *Famous South Coast pleasure resorts ...*, p.234.
5. 1975, p.70.
6. The place-name Eastbourne derives from the Bourne stream which has its source near St Mary's church, and is now almost completely hidden in culverts. The form 'Bourne' is found in Domesday Book, and 'Estbourne' (distinguishing it from Westbourne) appears by 1364. The local name for the old village remained 'Bourne', and this usage persisted until the end of the 19th century.
7. Vol. 1, p.296.
8. *c.*1810, p.54.
9. *Coast of Sussex* (1836), p.205.
10. Quoted by Parry, *op. cit.*, p.183.
11. *East Bourne Memories...*, p.52.
12. *Op.cit.*, p.198.
13. *Bygone Eastbourne*, p.77.
14. *Op. cit.*, p.200.

Some Dates in Eastbourne's History

1690	30 June: English and Dutch navies unsuccessfully engaged the French fleet off Beachy Head
1724	The Hon. Spencer Compton purchased Bourne (later Compton) Place
1747	Wreck of the prize ship *Nympha Americana* at Beachy Head.
1780	Arrival of George III's children to stay at the Round House
1787	First guide to Eastbourne published by James Royer
1792	300 French émigrés landed at Eastbourne
1795	Circulating library and billiard rooms opened at Sea Houses
1804	Construction of the Martello Towers begun
1806	Redoubt begun
1814	St Mary's schools opened in the Old Town
1816	William Figg's map of Eastbourne published
1822	Lifeboat and coastguard services set up
1834	Belle Tout lighthouse came into use
1839	Holy Trinity Chapel opened
1849	Branch railway from Polegate to Eastbourne opened
1851	Eastbourne Gas Company set up
1853	Disastrous wreck of the *Dalhousie* off Beachy Head
1856	*Eastbourne Chronicle* began publication
1858	Succession of the 2nd Earl of Burlington to the Dukedom of Devonshire
1858	Local Board set up
1859	Christ Church, Seaside, opened
1859	Eastbourne Waterworks Company formed
1859	*Eastbourne Gazette* first published
1863	Eastbourne Providential Dispensary opened in Devonshire Place
1864	William Leaf built the Workmen's Hall in Seaside
1866	Site of railway station moved
1867	Eastbourne College founded
1867	St Saviour's Church consecrated in South Street
1869	All Saints' Convalescent Home, Meads, opened
1871	Gowland's *Eastbourne Directory* first published (until 1925)
1872	Pier completed
1873	*Cavendish Hotel* opened
1874	Devonshire Park opened
1875	*Royal Sovereign* lightship established
1878	St Andrew's Presbyterian (URC) Church, designed by F.J. Barker, opened in Blackwater Road
1881	Eastbourne Electric Light Company formed
1881	South of England Grass Court Tennis Championships first held in Devonshire Park

1882	Royal Parade and sea wall completed
1883	Incorporation of the Borough of Eastbourne
1883	Theatre Royal and Opera House, Seaside, opened
1883	Princess Alice Memorial Hospital opened
1885	Ceylon Place Baptist Church built
1886	'Saffrons' (a field name) Cricket and Football ground opened
1886	20 October: Town Hall opened
1887	Royal Eastbourne Golf Course opened
1888	Willingdon railway station opened (renamed Hampden Park in 1903)
1891	Death of the 7th Duke of Devonshire
1891	Separate Eastbourne police force set up
1892	Borough set up committee to investigate possibility of constructing a harbour at Langney Point
1895	Ashes of Friedrich Engels buried at sea off Beachy Head
1898	William Terriss memorial lifeboat house built
1901	Hampden Park opened
1902	New Beachy Head lighthouse came into use
1902	Statue of William, 7th Duke of Devonshire, unveiled
1903	Death of Edna Lyall (Ada Ellen Bayly), novelist and emancipationist
1903	King Edward VII stayed at Compton Place
1903	Corporation omnibus service inaugurated
1904	Theatre Royal in Seaside renamed Royal Hippodrome
1904	Technical Institute (library and museum) opened
1906	Tivoli cinema opened in Seaside
1908	Death of the 8th Duke of Devonshire at Cannes
1911	Eastbourne became a County Borough and was enlarged to include Hampden Park
1911	Completion of St Michael's, Upperton Road (begun in 1900 and designed by G.E.S. Streatfield)
1912	P & O liner *Oceana* sank off Beachy Head in collision with the barque *Pisagua*
1912	New church of St Andrew's Norway (Willingdon) built
1921	*Eastbourne Herald* first published
1923	Towner Art Gallery opened by the Marquess of Hartington
1926	Chatsworth Estates Company set up
1927	All Saints' Church, Carlisle Road, burned down
1930	St Mary's Hospital opened (formerly Poor Law Infirmary)
1935	King George V and Queen Mary stayed at Compton Place
1937	Royal National Lifeboat Museum opened on Grand Parade
1938	Death of the 9th Duke of Devonshire
1938	New police headquarters opened in Grove Road
1938	Consecration of St Elizabeth's, Victoria Drive
1940	SS *Barnhill* bombed and set on fire off Beachy Head
1940	11 September: general evacuation of Eastbourne owing to threat of German invasion
1940	Willingdon House burned down
1944	Church of St Elizabeth partly destroyed by flying bomb
1948	Freedom of the Borough given to Winston Churchill
1949	Princess Margaret stayed at Compton Place
1949	New lifeboat, the *Beryl Tollemache*, launched
1949	Eastbourne College of Further Education founded
1950	Death of the 10th Duke of Devonshire at Compton Place

1957	Willingdon County Secondary School opened by Lord Hailsham
1960	Redoubt scheduled as an Ancient Monument
1961	Eastbourne Civic Society founded
1962	Royal Hippodrome Theatre purchased by Borough
1963	Congress Theatre, Devonshire Park, opened
1965	New Borough Library opened
1965	Polegate windmill purchased by Eastbourne Civic Society and reopened in working order in 1967
1966	Completion of South Cliff Tower, Meads
1968	Pier sold to Trust Houses Ltd., for £170,000
1970	Pier Theatre badly damaged by fire
1971	New *Royal Sovereign* light tower completed by the Danish firm Christiani & Nielsen at a cost of nearly two million pounds
1974	Foundation stone of T.G.W.U. Centre laid by Jack Jones
1974	Local Government reorganisation—Eastbourne lost County Borough status
1975	Bill to promote £50m development scheme (including harbour) at Langney defeated by Parliament
1975	Restoration of the Redoubt begun
1976	Phase I of new District Hospital opened
1981	Arndale Centre opened by the Duke of Devonshire
1981	Eastbourne College Big School gutted by fire
1985	Eastbourne Heritage Centre opened by the Civic Society
1988	Modified Eastbourne Harbour Bill passed
1990	Multiplex cinema opened by MGM at Crumbles Harbour Village
1990	Eastbourne voted 'Top Resort' by English Tourist Board
1990	By-election victory for Liberal Democrats—David F. Bellotte returned by 4,550 votes
1993	Crumbles Sovereign Harbour opened
1994	Greenwich light vessel automatic station established 25 miles southwest of *Royal Sovereign*

3 'East Bourne. Published by J. Sewell 32, Cornhill July 1793'—one of the earliest views of the Eastbourne area looking towards Pevensey Bay and Hastings. It was drawn by Nixon and engraved by Fitler, and appeared in the *European Magazine*.

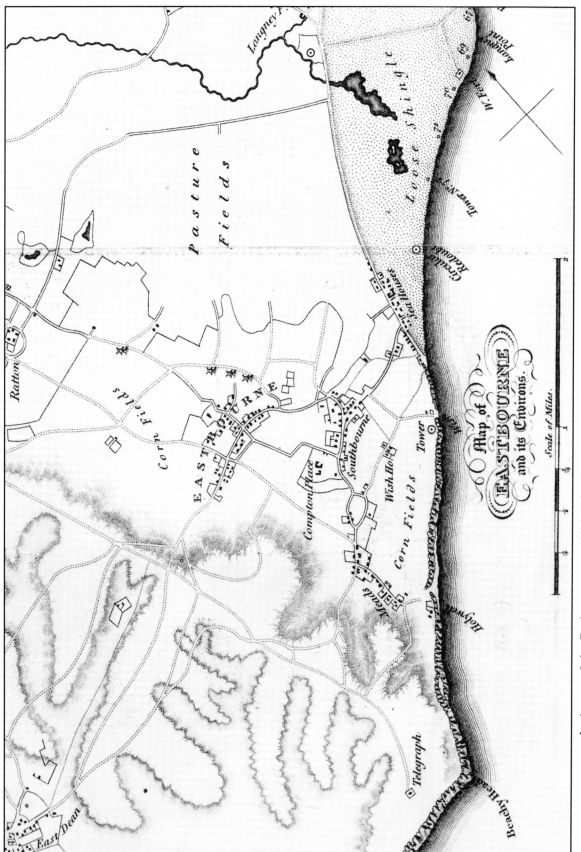

4   A map of the Eastbourne area published in 1819, showing the widely separated communities of the Old Town, Southbourne, Sea Houses and Meads.

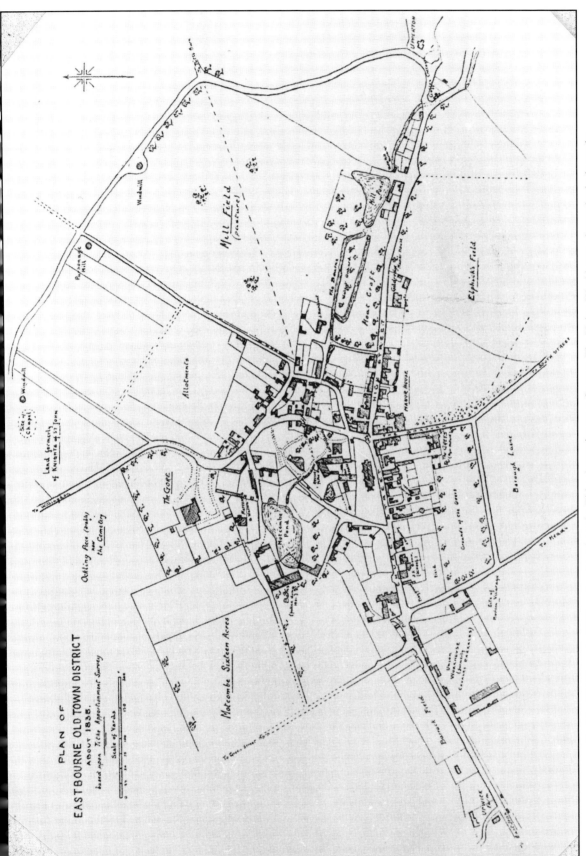

5 The Old Town in 1838; a plan based on the Tithe Apportionment Survey. The Union Workhouse, formerly the barracks, and J. Marchant's house (the Court House, now the *Rainbow Inn*) are shown.

6 An early photograph, *c*.1870, of the *Lamb Inn*, showing the building before the restoration of 1912.

7 The *Lamb Inn*, near St Mary's church, is a fine medieval-timbered building with a vaulted undercroft. In the early 19th century the inn provided an 'assembly room' and 'subscription ball room' for fashionable visitors to Sea Houses. The building's original timbering was revealed during restoration in 1912.

8 Church Street, Old Town, *c*.1900, with St Mary's church in the background.

9 A photograph of High Street in about 1900. The widening of the street began after the First World War and led to the permanent disfigurement of the Old Town. Among several historic buildings was the Old Dower House, an Elizabethan structure probably remodelled by Thomas Roots *c*.1700.

10 A self portrait of John Hamilton Mortimer, a notable artist of historic and romantic subjects. He was born at Eastbourne in 1740, and trained in London at the studio of Thomas Hudson (1701-1779). Mortimer, often referred to as the 'Salvator Rosa of England', was elected an R.A. in the year of his death in 1779.

11 The Old (Gildredge) Manor House at the lower end of High Street (The Goffs) is a building of medieval date with Elizabethan and Georgian additions. Much of it is possibly the result of a reconstruction carried out by Nicholas Gildredge in 1554. The Manor later passed to the Gilbert family who vacated it at the end of the 18th century and moved to the 'New Manor House', now the Towner Gallery. Interesting 15th-century mural paintings were uncovered at the Old Manor in 1957.

12 The Court House (now the *Rainbow Inn*), Moatcroft Road, *c*.1900. This 16th-century building is probably identical with, or on the site of, the Moot or meeting house of the Bourne Hundred. More recently known as Elm House, the photograph was taken by the Marchant family owners during the 19th century.

13 Davies Gilbert (1767-1839), a Cornishman (formerly Davies Giddy), assumed the name Gilbert on marrying Mary Anne, daughter of Charles Gilbert, Lord of Gildredge Manor in 1817; he thereby acquired a large estate. Davies Gilbert, who was a distinguished scientist, became High Sheriff of Cornwall in 1792-3, and President of the Royal Society, 1827-30.

14 The Manor House at the corner of Borough Lane is a fine example of 18th-century architecture, with a Tuscan-style porch. The house belonged successively to the Gildredge and Gilbert families, but in 1923 was purchased by the Borough and converted into the Towner Art Gallery. The name commemorates Alderman John Chisholm Towner, whose bequest of a collection of pictures together with £6,000 made the establishment of the Gallery possible. The building now includes a Local History Museum.

15 The old Jesus House (also known as 'Worge's House' after an 18th-century owner) which stood opposite St Mary's church until *c*.1895. The name derived from the building's original use as the Guild House of the local Brotherhood of Jesus, suppressed in the late 16th century. The site was the scene of an 'Urban Medieval Excavation Project' during 1977-78, organised by the Eastbourne Natural History and Archaeological Society.

16 The large medieval parish church of St Mary, *c*.1905. The massive early 15th-century tower is constructed of green sandstone from the Hastings area.

17 A sketch of the interior of St Mary's by Miss Emma Brodie. The view, dating from about 1840, is taken from the Sanctuary and shows (right) the original position of the Lushington Monument, now removed to the south aisle. Also shown are the fine 14th-century screens, the late Norman chancel arch, and the arcading with alternate round and octagonal piers.

18 The Lushington Monument in St Mary's church commemorates Henry, son of Henry Lushington, Vicar of Eastbourne from 1734 until 1779. He served in India during the Mutiny and survived the Black Hole of Calcutta only to be murdered later in 1863.

19 The Rectory Manor House or Old Parsonage near St Mary's is a good example of Tudor domestic architecture, probably erected by Hugh Rolfe, Diocesan Treasurer, 1519-1549. In 1846 it narrowly escaped demolition owing to dilapidation but survived and after occupation by pensioners was returned to the church and restored in about 1912.

20 Edgmond Hall, Church Street in about 1928, now Edgmond Evangelical Church. It was opened as a mission in 1872 by William Brodie, son of Alexander Brodie, Vicar of Eastbourne, 1809-28. William was converted by the preaching of Lord Radstock and became a leading member of the Open Brethren in 1870.

21 William Brodie, *c.*1890.

22 The Grays, *c.*1895. This ancient house stood in Borough Lane until 1910, and was occupied by the Vicars of Eastbourne during the 17th century when their official residence was ruinous. Later the house belonged to the Willard family, Major Nicholas Willard being Churchwarden, Chief Magistrate and Surveyor of Highways in the mid-19th century. This photograph shows the house after extensive rebuilding following a fire in 1853.

23 The Observatory at Northfield Grange, the residence of G.F. Chambers, who was a keen amateur astronomer and in 1867 published *Descriptive Astronomy, a General Book of Reference for All Classes of Readers.*

24 Part of the Star Brewery, which stood adjacent to the *Lamb Inn*. It was founded by William Hurst in 1777 and was formerly known as Hurst's, or the Old Town Brewery. The site was cleared in 1973 and a supermarket erected in 1983-4—a commercial rather than an environmental benefit to this historic area.

STAR BREWERY.

ALEX. HURST & CO.,

Brewers, AND Maltsters,

WINE & SPIRIT IMPORTERS,

EASTBOURNE.

BREWERY AND OFFICES:—
OLD TOWN.

BRANCH OFFICES AND STORES:—
64c, TERMINUS ROAD.

Families supplied with India Pale Ale, Bitter Beer and Nourishing Stout, in small Casks or Bottle.

PRICE LISTS MAY BE HAD ON APPLICATION.

ESTABLISHED 1777.

25 An advertisement for the Star Brewery, 1885.

26 The ruinous Ocklynge tower mill in 1930. The mill was erected *c*.1820 and demolished in 1934. Eastbourne was, as Hemming remarks, 'an area rich in windmills', there being at one time no less than 11 in the district, of which, sadly, only Polegate and Stone Cross now remain.

27   St John's or Hurst's tower mill *c*.1910. The mill was built by William Hurst in 1808, and when the cap jammed in 1917 it was run for a few years by a power engine. Much of the structure was demolished in 1951, but a portion still exists in Mill Road.

28 Sir Godfrey Kneller's portrait of Spencer Compton, Earl of Wilmington (1673-1743), who purchased Bourne Place in 1724. He was Speaker of the House of Commons from 1715 to 1727, and Lord Privy Seal in 1730.

29 Compton Place showing the north front. The house, originally called Bourne Place, was built by James Burton and passed to his son Edward in 1556. In 1724, it was sold by Sir Thomas Wilson to Spencer Compton (later the Earl of Wilmington), who enlarged and re-named it. The present appearance of the house dates from a further remodelling carried out in about 1800. As a seaside residence of the Dukes of Devonshire, Compton Place has several times provided accommodation for royal and other distinguished visitors to Eastbourne.

30 Summer scene at Compton Place in the 'Nineties'. A guide of the period noted that the house 'though presenting no striking architectural points' was, even so, 'an object of enthusiastic admiration to visitors'. Following the death of the 10th Duke of Devonshire at Compton Place in 1950, the house was closed (1952), and since 1954 has been occupied by a School of English, now called the Language Tuition Centre.

31 (*left*) The State bedroom at Compton Place, showing the fine moulded stucco ceiling executed in 1728 by Charles Stanley. The room was prepared by Spencer Compton in anticipation of a visit by George II, which in fact never materialised. The house also contains a first-floor gallery, surmounted by a square lantern decorated with elegant Rococo plasterwork.

32 (*right*) Louise, Dowager Duchess of Devonshire, was the daughter of Charles, Count von Alten of Hanover, and married the Duke of Manchester in 1852. Following the Duke's death she married the 8th Duke of Devonshire in 1892.

33 A view of the lower part of South Street in 1860.

34 South Street in about 1875. The buildings are: (left) Greystone Cottage; (centre) the small weather-boarded London Coach Office; (right) Filder's Cottages. Although no longer bearing any resemblance to old Southbourne, South Street, with its miscellany of late 19th-century architecture, is full of character and is now a conservation area.

Mr. & Mrs. Dormer.

THEATRE, EAST-BOURNE.

On THURSDAY Evening, OCT. 19, 1809, will be presented, a celebrated COMEDY, (written by R. B. Sheridan, Esq.) call'd,

THE

School for Scandal.

Sir Peter Teazle,	Mr. DORMER.
Sir Oliver Surface,	Mr. MORETON.
Joseph Surface,	Mr. RACKHAM.
Charles Surface,	Mr. AMTHOS.
Crabtree,	Mr. JONAS.
Sir Benjamin Backbite,	Mr. GEORGE.
Rowley,	Mr. GRIFFITH.
Careless, (with a Song)	Mr. BRANTON.
William,	Master RACKHAM.
Snake,	Mr. TAYLOR.
Mrs. Candour,	Mrs. NAYLOR.
Maria,	Mrs. BRANTON.
Lady Sneerwell,	Miss HOOPER.
And, Lady Teazle,	Mrs. DORMER.

END OF THE PLAY,
A favourite DANCE, by Miss HOOPER.
And, an IRISH SONG, by Mr. GRIFFITH.

To which will be added, the favourite musical Farce, (not acted here these six years) of

My Grandmother.

Sir Matthew Medley,	Mr. STACKWOOD.
Vapour,	Mr. AMTHOS.
Souffrance,	Mr. TAYLOR.
James,	Master RACKHAM.
Dicky Gossip,	Mr. JONAS.
Charlotte,	Miss HOOPER.
And, Florella, (My Grandmother)	Mrs. DORMER.

BOXES, 3s.——PIT and SLIPS, 2s.——GALLERY, 1s.
Tickets to be had at the Library; New-Inn; Lamb Inn; and of Mr. and Mrs. Dormer, at Mr. Adams's, carpenter, Bridges-Square; and at the Theatre, where Places for the Boxes may be taken.
Doors to be opened at SIX, and to begin at SEVEN o'clock.
No Person can be admitted behind the Scenes.

Nights of performing, will be Tuesdays, Thursdays, and Saturday.

Lewes: Printed by W. and A. Lee.

35 A playbill from the old Eastbourne theatre dated 19 October 1809. It is recorded that Thomas Dibden, when he belonged to the Folkestone Company, once acted at a theatre in the Southbourne area, very possibly the one in South Street. Plays were also given in the *Lamb Inn* assembly rooms in the early 19th century.

6 The old Theatre, South Street, which stood nearly opposite the Free Church, was erected around 1798, possibly by Charles Vine. Details of the theatre's history are uncertain but there is evidence of its sale by a Francis Gell for £400 in about 1800. By 1850 it had been converted into a builders' depot by Edward Maynard. It was later purchased by the Borough and demolished around 1885.

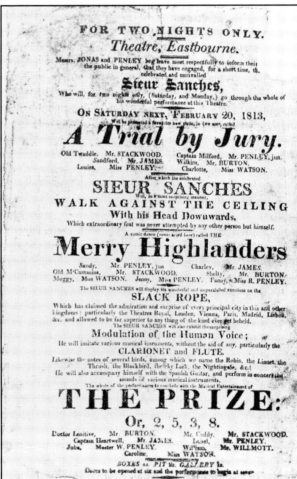

FOR TWO NIGHTS ONLY.

Theatre, Eastbourne.

Messrs. JONAS and PENLEY beg leave most respectfully to inform their the public in general, that they have engaged, for a short time, the celebrated and unrivalled

Sieur Sanches,

Who will, for two nights only, (Saturday, and Monday,) go through the whole of his wonderful performance at this Theatre.

ON SATURDAY NEXT, FEBRUARY 20, 1813,

Will be presented a favourite new piece, in two acts, called

A Trial by Jury.

Old Twaddle,	Mr. STACKWOOD,	Captain Milford,	Mr. PENLEY, jun.
Sandford,	Mr. JAMES.	Wilkins,	Mr. BURTON.
Louisa,	Miss PENLEY.	Charlotte,	Miss WATSON.

After which the celebrated

SIEUR SANCHES

Will, in a most surprising manner,

WALK AGAINST THE CEILING

With his Head Downwards,

Which extraordinary feat was never attempted by any other person but himself.

A comic dance (never acted here) called THE

Merry Highlanders

Sandy,	Mr. PENLEY, jun	Charley,	Mr. JAMES.
Old M'Cummins,	Mr. STACKWOOD,	Shelty,	Mr. BURTON.
Moggy,	Miss WATSON.	Jenny,	Miss PENLEY.	Fanny,	Miss R. PENLEY.

The SIEUR SANCHES will display his wonderful and unparalleled exertions on the

SLACK ROPE,

Which has claimed the admiration and surprise of every principal city in this and other kingdoms: particularly the Theatres Royal, London, Vienna, Paris, Madrid, Lisbon, &c. and allowed to be far superior to any thing of the kind ever yet beheld.

The SIEUR SANCHES will also exhibit the surprising

Modulation of the Human Voice;

He will imitate various musical instruments, without the aid of any, particularly the

CLARIONET and FLUTE.

Likewise the notes of several birds, among which we name the Robin, the Linnet, the Thrush, the Blackbird, the Sky Lark, the Nightingale, &c.

He will also accompany himself with the Spanish Guitar, and perform in concert the sounds of various musical instruments.

The whole of the performances to conclude with the Musical Entertainment of

THE PRIZE:

Or, 2, 5, 3, 8.

Doctor Lenitive,	Mr. BURTON.	Mr. Caddy,	Mr. STACKWOOD.
Captain Heartwell,	Mr. JAMES.	Label,	Mr. PENLEY.
Juba,	Master W. PENLEY.	William,	Mr. WILLMOTT.
Caroline,	Miss WATSON.		

BOXES 4s. PIT 2s. GALLERY 1s.

Doors to be opened at six and the performance to begin at seven.

7 Another playbill from the old Theatre, dated 20 February 1813.

38 Cooper's Brewery, South Street, *c.*1860. A brewery had occupied this site for many years, and was taken over by Robert Cooper from the Hurst family in 1845. Cooper erected new premises in Junction Road in 1870, when the old site was vacated.

39 The 'Eastbourne Artizan Dwellings 1891', and 'Central Court c.1879' form a nicely varied group of Victorian buildings in South Street. The Central Court (right) has modified Gothic detail and an attractive Tudoresque oriel bay over the main door.

40 Rose Cottage was a notable building in Grove Road, once belonging to Sir Arthur Piggott, Attorney General and M.P. for Arundel (died 1819). George F. Chambers recounts the local belief that it was haunted, and once sold for only £30 because of its reputation! The Cottage was demolished in 1882.

41 Grove Road in 1898, showing the fire station with a fire escape standing against a tall hose-drying tower, to the right of which is the old Vestry Hall.

42 The spectacular arch mounted by the local firemen to mark the visit of the Prince and Princess of Wales in June 1883.

43 The old fire station and solitary cyclist in Grove Road, *c.*1895.

44 Rural Grove Road in about 1877, showing the police station on the left. Eastbourne was policed by the County Force until 1892, when a separate force was established.

45 A photograph dating from about 1870 of the old *Squirrel Inn* (formerly Hartfield Farm House and later called the *Terminus Hotel* and the *Gilbert Arms*) which used to stand near the railway station.

46 Another view of the *Squirrel Inn* (also known as the *Gilbert Arms*) from an aquatint dated July 1858. The caption records that the bay-windowed room (left) was where the composer Sir William Sterndale Bennett (1816-1875) wrote *The May Queen*, when staying in Eastbourne in 1858.

47 Reginald J. Graham J.P., appointed first Chairman of the town's Local Board in January 1859.

48 Members of the Local Board displaying a fine array of top hats at the opening of the main sewer outfall at the Crumbles in 1866.

49 Terminus Road looking south-east in 1863. The road has become the town's main shopping street, and was laid out as a result of the coming of the railway in 1849 to provide a route from the station to the front. The road has now been made into a pedestrian precinct.

50 Oak Cottage, Terminus Road, *c*.1875. This site was strongly advocated as an alternative to Stocks Bank for the Town Hall at the time of Incorporation. The name 'Oak' is said to have originated from the owners' (the Pendrells) descent from the Boscobel farmer who sheltered Charles II after the battle of Worcester.

51 The Elms, which once stood at the corner of Susans and Seaside Roads, was built in 1714 as part of Susans Farm, and demolished in 1900. In the late 18th century the house was owned by James Royer, author of Eastbourne's first *Guide* published in 1787. Later the building was purchased by Mr. Graham who named it The Elms.

52 The south end of Cavendish Place, *c*.1900, showing late Regency-style bow fronts erected in the 1850s, reminiscent of C.A. Busby's designs in Brighton.

53 Stocks Bank, where the Town Hall now stands, *c.*1880. The choice of the site had led to argument in 1877, when the Chairman of the Local Board had considered that a town hall on the site 'would be a disgrace to Eastbourne'. As the name suggests, the village stocks were once situated here, and the area was also used as a fairground.

54 Laying the foundation stone of the Town Hall, 9 October 1884. The competition for designing the building was won by W. Tadman Foulkes of Birmingham, and the final cost was around £30,000. The stone was laid by Lord Edward Cavendish (left), and prayers were led by the Vicar, Thomas Pitman (right). In 1886, the town's invitation to Queen Victoria to open the Town Hall was declined.

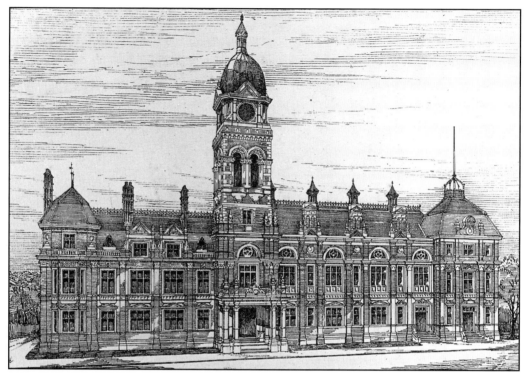

55 The newly completed Town Hall (by W.T. Foulkes) in 1886. The style was described as 'free Renaissance', and the asymmetry of the façade enhances the effect of this handsome Victorian building. The chiming clock by Gillett & Johnson was installed in 1892.

56 A group photograph taken on the occasion of the presentation of the Mace and Chain of Office to the Mayor and Corporation of Eastbourne on 21 April 1884. The Mace was given by Carew Davies Gilbert, and the Chain by the Duke of Devonshire.

57 The first Mayor (G.A. Wallis) and officers of the Borough in 1883, a commemorative group of portraits assembled at the time of Incorporation.

58 Lady Knill planting a commemorative tree in Gildredge Park, one of the events marking the 'acquisition of the rights and privileges of a County Borough' by Eastbourne, in June 1911. The group includes the Duke and Duchess of Devonshire and Sir John Knill, Alderman of the City of London, and Lord Mayor in 1909-10.

59 On 17 August 1901, following a public subscription, a bronze statue of William, 7th Duke of Devonshire, was unveiled by the Marquess of Abergavenny in Devonshire Place. It was executed by Sir William Goscombe John, and this sketch of the ceremony made by Arthur Garratt.

60 The memorial to the 2nd Battalion, Royal Sussex Regiment, was erected in 1904, and designed by Sir William Goscombe John (1860-1952). Cavendish Place in the background is where Friedrich Engels stayed at no. 4 on several occasions in 1893-4.

61 The War Memorial to the Eastbourne men who gave their lives in the two World Wars. The statue, which stands at the junction of Cornfield Road and Devonshire Place, was designed by Henry C. Fehr of South Kensington and unveiled by General Lord Horne on 10 November 1920.

62 The Round House, which stood near the Pier entrance (Sea Houses), was originally a horizontal windmill and was converted into a 'marine residence' in the mid-18th century. In 1780 the House was occupied by Prince Edward and other children of George III. The Round House was later threatened by sea encroachment and demolished in 1841. On the right is Field House.

63 A lithograph of Sea Houses, *c.*1820, showing the library and Mr. Webb's Baths, two important facilities of the early resort.

64 Marine Parade (Sea Houses) in about 1855 showing (right) Hopkins' circulating library. One of the original amenities provided for visitors to the resort, it was founded by George Fisher in 1784 and later owned by Thomas S. Gowland from 1862.

65 Gowland's old library just before demolition in 1948. T.S. Gowland died in 1923 and the firm closed in 1925 having moved by then to 52 Seaside Road.

66 Eastbourne sea-front near the present Grand Parade, from a drawing by Harriet Ogle in 1833. The Redoubt stands on the left.

67 Fishermen and their boats at Sea Houses, a print dating from 1834.

68 Colliers unloading at Eastbourne—an interesting sketch by Harriet Ogle, dated 25 September 1845.

69 Splash Point, from an old print dating from before the erection of the *Queen's Hotel* in 1880.

70 A recent photograph of Marine Parade showing (centre) all that remains of the old Sea Houses.

71 A print of the considerable damage sustained by the pier in the great gale of January 1877. Repairs were carried out by the designer, Eugenius Birch, and resulted in the replaced section being built at a higher level. This discrepancy is still visible, just north of the central Pavilion.

72 An old view of the pier, showing the original kiosks at the shore end. The pier was built during 1866-72 and designed by Eugenius Birch at a cost of £13,400, the first section being opened by Lord Edward Cavendish in June 1870. The contractors were J.E. Dowson & Head Wrightson.

73 An early seaplane east of the pier, *c*.1909. The photograph also provides an excellent view of the pierhead buildings, and on the extreme right the old pier bandstand, now removed.

74 The shore end of the pier, *c*.1926, showing the picturesque trio of kiosks which were replaced in the late 1940s. Behind is the large Music Pavilion, erected in 1924 at a cost of £15,000. Later the Pavilion became a dance hall, and since 1968 has been an amusement hall.

75 The pier, *c*.1930. The first pierhead pavilion, with a plain gabled roof, was erected in 1888 and replaced by an elaborate domed structure built in 1899-1901, designed by N. Ridley, costing £30,000. This pavilion, somewhat modified after fire damage in 1970, remains the one in use today. The midway games saloon was added in 1901.

76 A Salvation Army meeting below the *Burlington Hotel*, *c*.1898. Eastbourne's notable reputation for sabbatarianism was shattered by the Army's vigorous brass bands in the '90s, but efforts to subdue the 'nuisance' led to violence and were ultimately dropped.

77 The *Cavendish Hotel*, *c*.1890. The hotel was built in 1873 and enlarged nine years later, the architect being Thomas E. Knightley, who also designed the Queen's Hall, London. The east end of the building was severely damaged by bombing and has been reconstructed in modern style.

78 Holiday crowds on the Parade, *c*.1904. In the background is the Wish Tower.

79 A horse omnibus about to depart from the pier, *c.*1895.

80   The old *Rocket* coach outside the *Albion Hotel*, Marine Parade. A sketch from the *Daily Graphic* published during the coaching revival of the 1890s.

81   An old print of the *Grand Hotel* c.1890. For many years the hotel's famous orchestra broadcast light music from the Palm Court, led by such well-known musicians as Van Leir, Arthur Beckwith, Albert Sandler and Tom Jenkins.

82 An assemblage of Eastbourne 'characters' of the Victorian era, sketched for the *Daily Graphic* in December 1890.

83 A view of Eastbourne from the sea, *c.*1877, showing the original design of the pier.

84 Eastbourne, 1905. The leisured classes performing the ritual 'Sunday Parade' on the sea-front lawns with the Wish Tower in the background.

85 Charles Darwin (1802-82), the famous naturalist, stayed for a time at Sea Houses in the 1850s while working upon his *Origin of Species*.

36 Late Victorian beach scene just west of the pier.

37 Professor T.H. Huxley (1825-95), the famous scientist, lived in old age for a time at Meads. 'His principles', G.F. Chambers wrote, 'were so distasteful to me that I never sought his acquaintance, and had no nearer personal knowledge of him than that derived from sitting opposite him in a railway carriage!'.

88 (*right*) The Eastbourne Military Band with their conductor Mr. U. Giacomo, *c*.1919. On the left is the Grand Parade bandstand which was demolished in 1934.

89 (*below*) Edwardian promenaders on the sea-front. In the centre is the old 'bird cage' bandstand, erected in 1893 at a cost of £300 and replaced by the present Grand Parade Band Enclosure in 1934-5.

90 (*below*) Horse-drawn traffic along the Grand Parade, *c*.1900.

91 Eastbourne sea-front from the Wish Tower in the early 1900s. Note the almost impenetrable line of bathing machine along the sea's edge!

Feb. 1877.

2 Roller-skating in progress at the Floral Hall, Devonshire Park in 1877.

1879.

DEVONSHIRE PARK
AND
BATHS COMPANY, LIMITED,
EASTBOURNE.

ADMISSION ... ... SIXPENCE.
BATH CHAIRS ... ... ONE SHILLING.
A charge of 6d. is made for the use of Plimpton Skates.

	A Year.	6 Months.	1 Month.	Fortnight.
SUBSCRIPTION TICKET	40/- ...	30/- ...	15/- ...	10/-

FAMILY TICKETS.

	A Year.	6 Months.	1 Month.	Fortnight.
For 1st Subscriber	40/- ...	30/- ...	15/- ...	10/-
„ 2nd „	22/6 ...	17/- ...	12/6 ...	8/-
„ each subscription after	17/6 ...	12/6 ...	10/- ...	5/-

These Tickets are transferable only to a member of the holder's family or to friends being bonâ fide Visitors in the holder's house.

N.B.—Holders of Tickets are warned that the Tickets are liable to be forfeited if used for other than a member of the holder's family or a friend staying in his or her house.

SKATING RINKS.
THE INSIDE AND OUTSIDE RINKS
Cover Half-an-Acre of Skating Ground.

SKATING HOURS.—11 a.m. to 1 p.m., 4 p.m. to 6 p.m., 7.30 p.m. to 9.30 p.m.
SKATES CAN BE RESERVED.

Terms :—	A Year.	6 Months.	3 Months.	1 Month.	Fortnight.
	21/- ...	15/- ...	10/- ...	5/- ...	3/-

Skates can be re-rollered as often as wished.

A BAND ATTENDS THE RINK.

Clubs for Cricket, Croquet, Bowls, Archery, Lawn Tennis, Badminton,
Subsciption for Members to each Club, 5s. for the season.
☞ MEMBERS MUST BE SUBSCRIBERS.

Visitors can join either of these Clubs on giving satisfactory references.
The Board of Management reserve to themselves the right of naming certain days, should they see fit to do so, when Tickets will not be available.

SWIMMING BATHS FOR LADIES AND GENTLEMEN.
PRIVATE - BATHS FOR LADIES AND GENTLEMEN.

Any information required, or complaints to be made, address,
THOMAS HOLMAN,
Secretary.

3 An early advertisement giving details of activities at Devonshire Park.

94 Devonshire Park, *c.*1882. Some ten years later it was written of the Park that 'Among the many claims which Eastbourne puts forward for the favourable consideration of visitors ... none holds a higher place in the estimation of the *beau monde* than the Devonshire Park'. Undoubtedly the Park, especially during its early years, epitomised the secluded atmosphere and select tone which was the town's chief objective to maintain.

95 The Floral Hall, Devonshire Park in the late 1890s. The Hall, described as 'an elegant building in the Paxton Style', was the first to be erected in the Park, and became the venue for important functions in the town, as well as providing for roller-skating and dancing. It is now used as a small cabaret theatre.

76 Out for a spin! One of the facilities offered by Devonshire Park was the 'Bicycle Academy' which provided cycle proficiency lessons and was particularly recommended 'for ladies visiting Eastbourne and desirous to acquire the most necessary art of wheeling in correct style'.

77 The Indian Pavilion, Devonshire Park in 1910. This was an 'imported' building designed by T.E. Collcutt in 1892 and first erected for the Royal Naval Exhibition at Chelsea that year. Later it was re-assembled in the Park and used for refreshments and dressing rooms. The Pavilion survived until 1963, when it was demolished to make way for The Congress Theatre.

98 The Devonshire Park Theatre with its Italianate tower was designed by Henry Currey and opened on Whit Monday 1884 with a performance of T.W. Robertson's *David Garrick*. In 1903, much of the interior was remodelled by Frank Matcham.

99 The distribution of prizes at the Annual Amateur Athletic Sports in Devonshire Park, *c*.1896.

100   Part of the crowded Tournament Ground, Devonshire Park, *c*.1897.

101 A balloon ascent at the Eastbourne Schools Extension Bazaar in Devonshire Park, June 1895.

102 Tennis in Devonshire Park, *c.*1911. In 1897 Eastbourne Corporation began unsuccessful negotiations to purchase the Park, and later in 1912 and 1914 bills were promoted in Parliament to acquire the area but polls taken of ratepayers went against the move. It was not until 1931 that the Winter Garden was taken over, and 1946 when the old Devonshire Park Company was wound up.

103 The Duke of Devonshire's Eastbourne Orchestra with its conductor, Pierre Tass, *c.*1903. The group was formed in 1874 as the Devonshire Park Orchestra under Julian Adams, and later Norfolk Megone was conductor for some years. In 1922 a Municipal Orchestra was founded which continued until 1941.

104 Captain Henry G. Amers, conductor of the Eastbourne Municipal Orchestra from 1920 until his death in 1936. In 1923 he introduced an annual Musical Festival, which over the years enriched the cultural life of the town and led to visits by some notable musical personalities, including Sir Edward Elgar, Alexander Glazunov (1931) and Eric Coates.

105 A print of Beachy Head published in Royer's *Guide* in the late 1790s. The scenic splendour of the headland appealed to 18th-century taste—Richard Gough refers to it characteristically as 'promontory or frightful ridge', and it is said to have inspired the local artist John H. Mortimer.

106 A painting of the Battle of Beachy Head which took place in June 1690, when the combined English and Dutch fleets were defeated by the French Navy.

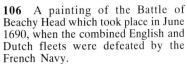

107 An 18th-century shipwreck at the foot of Beachy Head. From the distant past the headland has been a notorious hazard to shipping, but in spite of repeated complaints no permanent light was erected until 1829. Before that time a number of attempts had been made by local people, notably Jonathan Darby, Vicar of East Dean, to display signal lights during bad weather.

108   The *Thames*, an East Indiaman bound for China, was driven ashore at Langney Point in February 1822. She remained beached for three weeks, but after the removal of her cargo she was successfully repaired and refloated.

109   The wreck of the collier *Tally Ho*, on Boxing Day 1886. The ship was driven ashore with the loss of four crew while on her way from Sunderland to Littlehampton. She was owned by Banfield's of Brighton.

110 (*right*) The Eastbourne lifeboat, *William and Mary*, and crew in 1899. The town's first un-named boat was constructed in 1822 by a local builder named Simpson, and provided by John Fuller M.P., of Rose Hill. This boat was replaced in 1863 by the *Mary Stirling*, which was stationed near the Redoubt. In 1899 a No. 2 Station, the William Terriss Memorial Boat House, was opened at the Wish Tower and used until 1937, when it became a Lifeboat Museum.

111 (*below*) The fishermen of Eastbourne *en fête* for the visit of the Prince and Princess of Wales in June 1883.

112 (*below*) Beachy Head lighthouse under construction in 1901, showing the hoisting platform and tackle used to transport equipment and material from the cliff top.

113 The 'new' Beachy Head lighthouse from a photograph taken shortly after its completion in 1902. Work on the 153-foot tower began in July 1899, the foundations being sunk 18 feet into the solid chalk. Some 3,660 tons of Cornish granite were used in the construction.

114 Belle Tout lighthouse, *c*.1890. The building was superseded in 1902, and later became a private residence, belonging in the 1930s to the surgeon Sir John Purves. During the Second World War the lighthouse was severely damaged by gunnery practice, but was largely restored in 1955.

115 Inside the lantern of the Belle Tout lighthouse in 1884. The 'Belle Tout' (a Norman French term meaning a look-out) was built at the suggestion of John Fuller of Rose Green, and its erection was begun in 1832 by Trinity House, replacing a temporary light set up in 1829.

116 The old *Royal Sovereign* lightship was established in 1875 to mark the nearby shoals, and was replaced by a concrete light tower in 1971. A Greenwich light vessel automatic station, 25 miles to the south west, began operating in 1994.

117 The frigate HMS *Eastbourne* (2,560 tons) was launched in December 1955, and commissioned in January 1958. Built by Vickers-Armstrong (Tyne), she was later used for training at Rosyth until she was scrapped in 1986.

118 Crowds salvaging tinned food and other cargo from the SS *Barnhill* in 1940. The ship was attacked by German aircraft off Beachy Head and later ran aground.

119 The old Eastbourne Artillery Volunteers on the ramparts of the Redoubt, *c*.1890.

120 Troops encamped in the Redoubt, *c*.1890. The fortress is Eastbourne's finest relic of the Napoleonic era, and was begun in 1806 as part of the coastal defences, being provided with a garrison of about two hundred men and 11 guns. Below the parapet is a series of vaulted chambers (casemates) around an open central parade area. The Redoubt became virtually redundant in 1859, but was in occasional use until 1900. In 1925 the fortress was purchased by the town and opened to the public.

121 The devastated Martell Tower No.71 after its use as a target by a battery of new guns designed by Sir W.G Armstrong in August 1860. The practice took place in the presence of the Duke of Cambridge, the battery being mounted near the St Anthony Hill Tower, Langney.

122 Wish Tower (Martello Tower No.73) from an old print. The Tower was built in 1804 as part of the coastal defences against Napoleon, and its establishment was an officer and 24 men with a heavy cannon mounted on top. After the war it was disused until 1830 when coastguards occupied it for a time. In 1883 the Tower was leased from the War Office by the town, and became the home of the Hollobon family who ran it as a small geological museum.

123 Holiday-makers around the Wish Tower, *c.*1912. The name 'Wish' derives from the once marshy area called the 'wish' or 'wash' situated nearby, where the old Shomer Dyke entered the sea. During the Second World War the Tower became part of a defensive gun emplacement, but in 1954 was threatened with demolition when the site was considered for a projected Conference Hall. In 1960 it was restored and a 'sun lounge' built nearby. Later (1970) the Tower was opened as a Coastal Defence Museum.

124 The opening of the Eastbourne branch railway on 14 May 1849. From 1846, when the line reached Polegate, the town was connected to the railhead by a horse-omnibus service owned by the landlord of the *Anchor Inn*. The first train, carrying a party of officials, arrived to the strains of a brass band shortly after midday, when a large company was entertained to lunch in the garden of Orchard Farm.

125 Eastbourne's third railway station, *c.*1876.

126 Eastbourne railway station, *c*.1895. The original wooden station was a little to the west of the present site, the move being necessitated by the laying out of Upperton Road. A new station was opened in 1866, and a third in 1872, this being rebuilt to form a fourth in 1886, which remains in use today.

127 An old view of the Eastbourne branch line. The locomotive is a Craven 'South London Tank', No. 230, built at the Brighton Works in 1866.

128 Another steam locomotive bearing a local place-name was the *Willingdon*, a Neilson D I class no. 255. The photograph was taken at Eastbourne in 1881. The first steam locomotive to bear the name *Eastbourne* was the Stroudley 'B' or Gladstone Class no. 183 built in 1889. She was later renumbered SR B183 and scrapped in 1929.

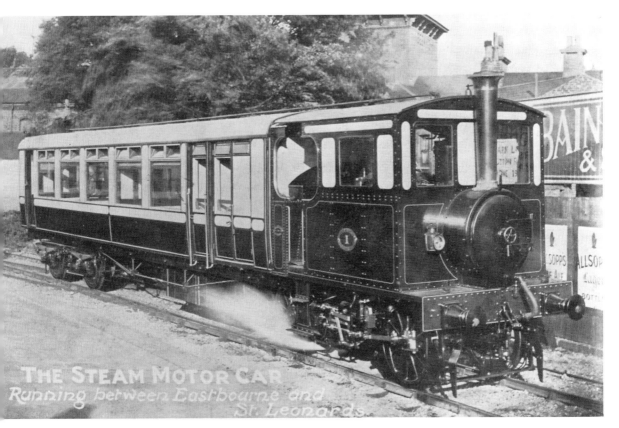

THE STEAM MOTOR CAR
Running between Eastbourne and
St Leonards.

129 (*above*) In September 1905, the
L.B.S.C.R. introduced a 'Motor Train' service
between Eastbourne and St Leonards, operated
by four units; two powered by steam and two
by Daimler petrol engines. The steam unit No.
1, shown here, cost £2,145 and was built by
Bayer and Peacock. They continued running
until 1912, although the performance was never
very satisfactory because of inadequate boiler
size.

130 (*left*) During the years 1930-35 the
engineer R.E.L. Maunsell designed the well-
known 'Schools' class 4-4-0 steam locomotives
for the Southern Railway. Pictured here is the
engine *Eastbourne* built as E914 (later C30914)
in December 1932, and named after Eastbourne
College. After nearly thirty years' service she
was scrapped in July 1961.

131 Eastbourne's first 'motor' omnibus, together with a group of Aldermen and Councillors in 1904. The Eastbourne Corporation Omnibus Service claims to be the first municipal transport undertaking ever formed.

132 Canon Thomas Pitman, Vicar of Eastbourne, 1828-90. He was described by G.F. Chambers as 'a notable personality ... essentially a "strong" man, and if he had not been a parson, he had some qualifications for being a Judge of the High Court'.

133 An engraving of Holy Trinity Church, designed by Decimus Burton in 1837-39, as a Chapel of Ease to St Mary's. In 1847 it became a parish church, and subsequently underwent a number of enlargements and alterations which considerably changed its appearance. Of Burton's original design only the nave arcade and the re-sited and re-built tower remain.

134 Christ Church, Seaside, Eastbourne was designed by Benjamin Ferrey and opened in 1859. The chancel has a memorial window to Princess Alice, daughter of Queen Victoria, who patronised the church during her stay at Eastbourne in 1878.

135 St John's, Meads, from a print of c.1870. The church was designed by a local architect, H. Ewan Rumble, in 1868-9, and in 1942 all but the tower was destroyed by bombing. The spire was removed during the rebuilding and restoration work in the 1950s.

36 St John's, Meads, as it appears today, showing the new nave designed by A.E. Matthew and erected in 1954-57. The modern style Baptistry with contemporary stained glass was added in 1962.

37 St Saviour's, South Street was described by Goodhart-Rendel as 'a very noble church', and its graceful 175-foot spire greatly enhances the town centre. The church was founded by George Whelpton in 1867 on land given by the Duke of Devonshire.

138 Laying the foundation stone of a new church—both an important and commonplace event during the Victorian period. This photograph shows the ceremony at All Saints', Carlisle Road on 1 November 1877.

139 The Italian Romanesque style of All Souls', Susans Road makes it one of the most striking Victorian churches in Sussex. It was designed by the London architect A.P. Strong and erected in 1882 with money provided by Lady Victoria Wellesley, great-niece of the Duke of Wellington. The fabric includes elaborately moulded terracotta dressings, and the campanile is 83 feet high.

140 The basilica-style interior of All Souls' Church. The seven-bay arcade is constructed from Horsham stone, supported on columns which have Byzantine-style capitals of varying design. The walls have decorative banding in red and yellow brick.

141 The former church of St Anne, Upperton Gardens was designed by C. Haddon in 1881, and described as 'the Church of the Gilbert Estate in the aristocratic Upperton district'. Gutted by incendiary bombs during the war, St Anne's was demolished in 1955.

142 St Peter's church which used to stand at the corner of Meads and Grandville Roads. Although a listed building, it was declared redundant and later demolished in 1971. St Peter's began as a temporary Chapel of Ease to St Saviour's on a site behind the Town Hall in 1878; but in 1894 a new church (illustrated) was erected. Both churches were designed by Henry Currey.

143 The church of Our Lady of Ransom, near the Town Hall, was designed by Frederick A. Walters in 1899 and the tower added in 1912. The first Roman Catholic Mission named Stella Maris, was established by Father Charles P King in Terminus Road in 1867.

144 A print dated 1863 showing (left) the Cavendish Place Calvinistic Independent Chapel. The chapel was opened in 1857, and supported mainly by a local farmer named Gorringe. The congregation had begun worship in 1823 in a converted bakehouse and stables, built by a Mr. Grace and known as 'Mr. Grace's Chapel'.

145 The attractive red brick and Bath stone Baptist Church in Ceylon Place was opened in 1886. Baptist worship began in Eastbourne with services held in Leaf Hall in August 1870, and the following year an 'iron' Tabernacle was erected on the present site, with George H. Sandwell as first Minister. As shown here, the church was badly damaged by bombing in 1943, and re-opened in 1948, with some modification of the interior design.

146 A church outing about to start from the Ceylon Place Baptist Church, c.1895.

147 The Central Methodist Church, Pevensey Road was designed by a local architect, Carlos Crisford, and opened in 1908. The first Methodist worship in Eastbourne began in 1803 at Sea Houses, organised by soldiers stationed in the area. In 1810 a chapel was established in Grove Road by the Rev. Robert Pilter, and used until 1864 when the Pevensey Road site was first occupied.

148 An old print of Langney Priory. The building was possibly a grange of the Cluniac Priory at Lewes, and incorporates a chapel and also a refectory with dormitory above. The area surrounding the Priory has been much affected by housing development since the war.

149 The attractive old infant school building which stands in Meads Road. For many years it was known as 'Lady Burlington's School', and the cartouche inscription in the north gable states that it was 'erected by Blanche, Countess of Burlington' in 1836. The school was briefly attended by George Meek—'the Bath-chair man'—in 1874. Meek was born in Eastbourne and became an eloquent socialist, his views attracting the attention of H.G. Wells who wrote a preface to Meek's autobiography in 1910.

150 The opening of the third day of the Eastbourne schools extension bazaar by Viscountess Cantelupe in Floral Hall, Devonshire Park on 27 June 1895.

151 Clifton House boys school, South Street (near St Saviour's) was one of the most successful private schools in the town. It was founded in 1836, and for many years published a school magazine *The Eastbourne Cliftonian*. In 1880 the fees per annum were 12 guineas for day pupils, and 50 guineas for boarders.

52 An early photograph of Eastbourne College and the surrounding area taken in 1872 from the newly completed tower of St Saviour's Church. At the top right can be seen the isolated hamlet of Meads and St John's Church, which, as J.F. Chambers remarked, 'at that time occupied an open waste, and seemed nowhere'.

153 (*right*) Eastbourne College, the west front. The College was founded by a local doctor, Charles C. Hayman, and first occupied premises in Spencer Road, where the school opened on 20 August 1867 with 15 boys. The first headmaster was the Reverend James R. Wood. In 1870 the erection of school buildings on the present site began, and incorporated Larkfield House, formerly owned by Charles Rawdon. The foundation stone was laid by Lady Cavendish on 30 July 1870.

154 (*below*) School House, Eastbourne College, from a print of about 1872. The design of the first range of buildings (1870-78), including the chapel nave, was in a Gothic style and carried out by the Duke of Devonshire's architect Henry Currey.

55 The interior of Eastbourne College Chapel in 1903. The chapel was dedicated by the Bishop of Chichester on 20 June 1874, and designed by Henry Currey. The chancel was added in 1889, and the aisles in 1929.

156 Eastbourne College War Memorial Tower from t[ ]
south east. The War Memorial building was opened on 28 Ju[ ]
1925 by General Sir Charles Hartington, and designed in
Tudor style by Sydney Tatchell and G.C. Wilson. The Tow[ ]
is flanked to the south by the Devonshire Wing, and to t[ ]
north by the Arnold (headmaster, 1924-29) Wing.

157 Interior view of Big School, Eastbourne College, *c.*192[ ]
Designed by W. Hay Murray in 1909, the building was gutte[ ]
by fire in November 1981 and later restored.

158 The old Technical Institute, Grove Road, *c*.1912.
The building was designed by P.A. Robson, and opened
by the Dowager Duchess of Devonshire in August 1904.
The Institute housed the town's public library and
museum and was destroyed by bombing in the Second
World War. The site is now occupied by the new Library
and Corporation offices built in 1962-64 at a cost of
£158,000.

159 John Henry Hardcastle, F.L.A., Eastbourne's first
Borough Librarian, 1896-1933. Following the adoption
of the Public Libraries Acts, the old Vestry Room was
used as temporary premises from 7 July 1896. An earlier
attempt to adopt the Acts was frustrated by opposition
from local booksellers in 1871.

160 All Saints' Hospital, Meads, was begun in 1867 from designs by Henry Woodyer (1816-96), and opened two years later. The buildings, which were enlarged some 20 years later, form an interesting group in the Gothic Revival style of architecture.

161 The Reverend Mother Harriet (Harriet Brownlow Byron), founder of All Saints' Convalescent Home, Meads, in 1867. In 1851, Mother Harriet had established the Anglican Community of All Saints' Sisters of the Poor at All Saints', Margaret Street in London.

162 The striking interior of All Saints' Hospital Chapel, designed by Henry Woodyer in 1874. The style shows the influence of William Butterfield (Woodyer's master) in the polychrome effects of brick, stone and marble and geometrical tiling.

163 The young Princess Alice, second daughter of Queen Victoria, afterwards Duchess of Saxony and Grand Duchess of Hesse-Darmstadt. In 1878, the Princess and her husband made a very popular stay in Eastbourne, and the town was deeply shocked by the Princess's premature death from diphtheria later the same year.

164 The old Princess Alice Memorial Hospital, Carew Road, designed by T.W. Cutler (Bloomsbury) in the 'Queen Anne Style', was opened in 1883 by the Prince and Princess of Wales. The building commemorated the young Princess who died, aged 35, the same year as she had stayed in Eastbourne, 1878.

165 The Prince and Princess of Wales with other guests at the reception held at Compton Place after the opening of the Princess Alice Memorial Hospital in June 1883.

166 Leaf Hall, Seaside. The building was erected in 1864 as a 'Workmen's Hall' by a local philanthropist, William Leaf, on land given by the Duke of Devonshire. The inscription on the foundation stone records that the Hall's purpose was 'to promote the social, moral and spiritual welfare of the working classes'. The Hall was designed by a local architect, R.K. Blessley.

167 The north-east end of Meads Road showing (left) Caffyns Garage (on the corner) and Saffrons Rooms, built in 1910 and a pleasant example of the architecture of that period. Caffyns, one of Eastbourne's most notable firms, was founded by Percy T. Caffyn in 1902, and now has branches in several towns. Percy Caffyn's two sons Edward and Sydney have had distinguished careers, both receiving knighthoods. Sir Sydney Caffyn was Mayor of Eastbourne in 1956-58.

168 The Royal Hippodrome, Seaside Road was purchased by the Borough in 1962, but after financial losses closure was threatened in 1989. A Hippodrome Trust then took over and since 1991 Matthews Productions has successfully run the theatre which has undergone restoration.

169 Advertisement for the Theatre Royal and Opera House (Royal Hippodrome) in 1887. The leading theatre architect C.J. Phipps (1835-1897) was co-proprietor and designer of the building in 1883.

170 The old Tivoli cinema, Seaside Road. Built as the Mutual Improvement Society's hall in 1879, it became a cinema c.1907, later called Mansell's Picture Hall and then the Tivoli from 1916. It closed in 1982 and is now Shimmers leisure centre.

171 A drawing of the auditorium designed by the famous theatre architect Frank Matcham for the Eastbourne Picture Palace (later the Elysium, now Mecca Bingo, Seaside) in 1914. Much of the decorative work is still intact.

ELYSIUM
The Supreme Cinema
(Established 1918)

In every way up-to-date.

Sanitary arrangements certified **perfect.**

Up-to-date Ventilation.

REFINED PROGRAMME,
6 to 10.30 p.m.
MATINEES DAILY, 2.30 p.m.
MUSIC BY THE ELYSIUM TRIO

PIPE ORGAN
VARIETY TURNS.

Seats can be booked without extra charge.

---

238 SEASIDE.

Phone **43.** E. CHAPMAN,
Manager.

172 Advertisement for the Elysium, 186 Seaside in 1923. Opened as the Eastbourne Picture Palace in 1914 it became the Elysium in 1918, the Gaiety in 1937 and then the Classic in 1968, closing to become Mecca Bingo in 1974.

173 The surviving façade of the old Central Hall Electric Theatre at 56 Seaside Road. Opened in about 1908, it became the Manhattan in 1962-3 and then Star Bingo in 1970.

174 The green domed Deco-style Luxor cinema, Pevensey Road opened in April 1933, designed by J. Stanley Beard, F.R.I.B.A. Later acquired by Union (1936) then ABC (1938), the cinema was finally owned by Cannon before closing in 1991.

175 Gildredge Road under enemy air attack in September 1940. In the background can be seen the Town Hall tower and, in the middle distance, Emmanuel Church (an 'iron church'), which used to stand at the corner of Hyde and Calverly Roads until it was demolished in the late 1940s.

176 A major post-war development in Eastbourne was the erection of The Congress Theatre in Devonshire Park, opened in 1963. The building, intended to make the town competitive as a conference centre, was designed by Bryan and Norman Westwood & Partners, costing about £400,000, and has brick relief decoration on the north wall by Eric Peskett.

177 The new Transport and General Workers' Union Holiday and Conference Centre, costing upwards of three million pounds, was opened in Grand Parade by Jack Jones, CH on 9 September 1976. The building was designed by White & Traviss and stands on the site occupied for many years by the *Sea View Hotel*.

78 The Arndale Centre (1981) comprising 70 units was designed by Percy Gray and Leslie Jones and Partners (Poole), and has increased the already high reputation of Eastbourne as a shopping centre. The two entrances open into the pedestrianised section of Terminus Road.

Select Bibliography

Allom, V.M., *Ex Oriente salus: a centenary history of Eastbourne College* (Eastbourne College, 1967)

Armstrong, Robert, *Wings Over Eastbourne* (Eastbourne, Sound Forum, 1979)

Becket, T.R., *Front Line Eastbourne: an illustrated record of a famous holiday resort under enemy air assault, and a tribute to the stout-hearted residents who kept the flag flying* (Eastbourne, T.R. Becket Ltd., 1945)

Bickley, Francis L., *The Cavendish Family* (Constable, 1911)

Biggs, Howard, *The Sound of Maroons: the story of Life-Saving Services on the Kent and Sussex Coasts* (Lavenham, Terence Dalton, 1977). Chapter 7: Beachy Head, Eastbourne, pp. 116-126

Bourdillon, F.W., *Beachy Head*: a paper read before the Eastbourne Natural History Society (Eastbourne, Parsons & Towers, 1894)

Budgen, Reverend Walter, *Old Eastbourne: its Church, its Clergy, its People* ... (Frederick Sherlock Ltd., 1912)

Chambers, George F., 'Contributions towards a history of East-bourne' in *Sussex Archaeological Collections*, vol. 15 (1862), pp. 119-137

Chambers, George F., *East Bourne Memories of the Victorian period, 1845 to 1901* ...(Eastbourne, V.T. Sumfield, 1910)

Chambers, George F., *A Handbook for East-Bourne, Seaford* ... 11th edn. (Eastbourne, Keay, Leach, 1879)

Clarke, John, *History of the Eastbourne Medical Society 1883-1983* (The Society, 1983)

Clunn, Harold, *Famous South Coast pleasure resorts past and present* (T. Whittingham, 1929). Eastbourne, pp. 227-261

Cooper, Robert, *Reminiscences of Eastbourne* (Eastbourne, R. Cooper, 48 Grove Road, 1903)

Donne, James, 'Ducal Eastbourne', *Sussex Life*, Vol. 4 (March 1968), pp. 20-22

Eastbourne & District Joint Town Planning Advisory Committee, *Eastbourne & District Regional Planning Scheme: a report prepared for the* [Committee] ... *by Adams, Thompson & Fry, Town Planning Consultants* ... (Eastbourne, 1931)

Eastbourne Local History Society, *The 1841 Census for the Parish of Eastbourne, Sussex* (1990)

Eastbourne Public Libraries, *Catalogue of the Local Collection comprising books on Eastbourne and Sussex* (Eastbourne, Public Library, 1956)

East Sussex County Planning Department, *Eastbourne Borough Area Profile September 1975* (ESCC, 1975)

Eddison, Edwin, *The Guide to Eastbourne with a description of its neighbourhood* (Eastbourne, Charles H. Law, *c*.1866)

Fovargue, H.W. (ed.), *Municipal Eastbourne: a selection from the proceedings of the Town Council, 1883-1933* (Eastbourne, 1933)

Giddey, Canon (William) Denys, *The Story of All Saints' Hospital Eastbourne* (Eastbourne, All Saints' Hospital, *c*.1974)

Godfrey, Walter H., 'The Old Dower House, Eastbourne', *Sussex Archaeological Collections*, vol. 85 (1945), pp. 2-10

Goodwin, John E., *Eastbourne Redoubt* (Worthing, J.E. Goodwin, 1976)

Goodwin, John E., *Fortifications of the South Coast: the Pevensey, Eastbourne and Newhaven defences 1750-1945* ... (JJ Publications, 1994)

Gowans, Linda M., *The Story of Caffyns From 1865*, 2nd edn. (Eastbourne, 1989)

Gowland, T.S., *The Guide to Eastbourne revised and corrected*, 12th edn. (Eastbourne, T.S.

Graham, Reginald J., *Eastbourne recollections: magisterial and personal* (Eastbourne, E.B.R. Holloway, 1888)

Hardy, N.W. (ed.), *Eastbourne 1939-1945. With a section dealing with the preparations in Eastbourne from 1936-1939* (Eastbourne, Strange the Printer, 1946)

Heape, R. Grundy, *Buxton under the Dukes of Devonshire* (Robert Hale Ltd., 1948)

Heatherly, John, *A Description of East-Bourne and its Environs; in the County of Sussex ...* (Eastbourne, printed for John Heatherly, 1819)

Heys, Geoffrey, *Early Settlement in Eastbourne* (Eastbourne, 1980)

Hills, Ann and Hills, Nicholas, 'The Old Manor House, Eastbourne', *Sussex Notes and Queries*, Vol. 17 (1968), pp. 78-82

Humphrey, George, *Wartime Eastbourne: the Story of the most raided town in the South-east* (Beckett Features, 1989)

Knopp, B.B., *In Season Out of Season: the Story of Cavendish Place Chapel Eastbourne* (Eastbourne, 1980)

Meek, George (of Eastbourne), *George Meek Bath-chair man ... with an introduction by H.G. Wells* (Constable, 1910)

Miller, V., *Norway Notes (and the church of St. Andrew, Seaside Eastbourne)* (Eastbourne, 1986)

Milton, John, *Centenary History of Royal Eastbourne Golf Club* (1987)

Morris, Jeff and Hendy, Dave, *The Story of the Eastbourne Lifeboats* (Eastbourne, 1981)

PBN Publications, *Index to the 1914-1918 War Memorial of Eastbourne ...* (1990). Typescript

Reed, T., *The Fishermen and Boatmen of Eastbourne* (Eastbourne Local History Society, 1979-80)

Roper, F.C.S., *Flora of Eastbourne ...* (John Van Voorst, 1875)

(Royer, James), *Eastbourne, being a Descriptive Account of that Village, in the County of Sussex, and its environs. Addressed by permission, to their Royal Highnesses, Prince Edward and the Princesses Elizabeth and Sophia. Second Edition ...* (Printed at the Philanthropic Reform, for Hookham, Bond-street; and Wigstead, Charing-cross, 1799)

Sharpin, I.M. and Williams, C.F., *A Postal History of Eastbourne, 1750-1972* (Eastbourne, 1972)

Spears, Harold D., *Some of the street names of Eastbourne with notes on their historical associations* (Eastbourne, Eastbourne Local History Society, 1973)

Spencer, Dave, *Eastbourne Bus Story* (Middleton Press, 1993)

Stevens, Lawrence, *A Short History of Eastbourne*, 2nd. edn. (Eastbourne Local History Society, 1987)

Sutton, Thomas, *The Eastbourne Roman villa, with a supplement by Lawrence Stevens and Richard Gilbert* (Eastbourne, 1973). Reprinted with additions from the *Sussex Archaeological Collections*, Vol. 90 (1952)

Tipping, H., Avray, 'Compton Place, Sussex', *Country Life*, September 1916, pp. 266-273, 294-303

Walkley, Victor G., *A Church set on a hill: the story of Edgmond Hall, Eastbourne, 1872-1972* (Eastbourne, Upperton Press, 1972)

Whatmore, Father Leonard E., *The Story of Our Lady of Ransom, Eastbourne* (Lewes, W.E. Baxter Limited, 1978)

Wilson, D. Dunn, *From Seahouse to Central: a Short Account of 'The People Called Methodists'* (Eastbourne, 1978). Typescript.

Wilton, John and Smith, John, *Eastbourne in Old Picture Postcards*, 2 vols. (SB Publications, 1990-91)

Wolseley, Viscountess, 'Compton Place Eastbourne', *Sussex County Magazine*, Vol. 2 (1928)

Woodford, Cecile, *Eastbourne in Old Photographs* (A. Sutton, 1989)

Wright, J.C., *Bygone Eastbourne* (Spottiswoode, 1892)

Young, Kenneth, *Music's great days in the spas and watering-places* (Macmillan, 1968). Includes: 'Eastbourne: the Duke and the Municipality', pp. 149-169

EDMUND EVANS. S.